PRAISE FOR VIEW FROM THE OTHER SIDE

I am undone, says the speaker in the first poem of Betsy Snider's lush and intimate journey *View From the Other Side*, and at once we are in the thrall of a remarkable energy. Snider's language is fueled by this energy, this force, defined by continual movement—probing wider, diving deeper, until nothing less than a complete metamorphosis is achieved.

Richly threaded with themes, these poems probe and prod in search of god, of self. Water as the element of transformation holds all these threads together. The section titled Ars preces—the art of prayer—stops the heart. Compressed and untitled, these lyrics recall Hopkins' praise of his god, full of fury and passion for a divinity of human dimension. But instead of Hopkins finding god in *dappled things*, Snider laments the time she thought *god would melt on my tongue*, and now muses that *perhaps god tastes of ash, smoke / born on the wind*.

While these poems honor and celebrate life fully lived, they also challenge the very idea of an inevitable end. In the true sense of metamorphosis, transformation by its nature continues on. She writes: *The sheet is lifted over my slack face. / I dive deep into the lake, / touch the sandy bottom / and surge to the surface / aflame.* Surely this is divinity in its most intense articulation.

> — Pam Bernard, poet, educator and author of the verse novel,
> *Esther* published by CavanKerry Press

These are poems of yearning, of searching—for safety, for connection, for a higher power (if one exists). Drawing from the depths of memories of a child "bound" to her uncle "in silence and in shame" and a "young girl who thought she was called by god" to a silence imposed by life within a convent, *View from the Other Side* breaks into speech and song, looking fear ("night's quietest sound") in the face and creating a tie to the world through nature—a daily swim beginning every spring just after ice-out; hours spent on trails surrounded by hemlock, birches, and bees. "Maybe god /tastes of ash," writes Betsy Snider, but in her dreams she sings of blessings, and mercy is "buried deep / in the anvil of my ear."

> — Meg Kearney, author of *Home By Now*, winner of the
> PEN New England Award for Poetry

At lunchtime, I opened Snider's manuscript for a quick peek. Fifteen poems later, I realized I had not touched my lunch. Add a touch of Mary Oliver, and this tells all one needs to know about the vividness of Snider's imagery and its metaphorical leaps. Too often poets run up to the cliff edge and then back-off, take a safe route down. In the opening and closing sections of this book, Snider, again and again, sprints to the edge and leaps. In all leaps into the unknown, we never know quite what will happen when gravity brings us to earth as in "Memory Box, IV": "The lake is a perfect mirror . . . .//The old woman crosses a bridge/to the child who waits in a shadow."

Sometimes the landing brings deep pain, sometimes deep joy, sometimes solemn silence. But regardless where the landing, one is better for having risked the leap.

— Rodger Martin, author of *The Blue Moon Series* from Hobblebush Press and Co-editor, The Granite State Poetry Series

When lesbianism could have meant spiritual death for this former nun, Betsy Snider left the convent to seek the spiritual rebirth she needed to heal from her childhood trauma and loss of innocence. In *View from the Other Side* the biographical transcends mere storytelling to reach this alternative and equally valid spiritual place, and Snider tells this with startling imagery and a delicate and insightful poignancy. A famous Catholic poet (Billy Collins) once wrote, "To see life through the lens of death is to approach the condition of gratitude for the gift (or simply the fact) of our existence." Snider has found that gratitude and much more in these poems.

— Tim Mayo, author of *Thesaurus of Separation*, Finalist for the 2017 Eric Hoffer Book Award & the 2017 Montaigne Medal.

VIEW FROM THE OTHER SIDE

Poems by
Betsy Snider

BLUE LIGHT PRESS ❖ 1ST WORLD PUBLISHING

1ST WORLD
PUBLISHING

SAN FRANCISCO ❖ FAIRFIELD ❖ DELHI

View From the Other Side

BLUE LIGHT PRESS
www.bluelightpress.com
bluelightpress@aol.com

1ST WORLD PUBLISHING
PO Box 2211
Fairfield, IA 52556
www.1stworldpublishing.com

BOOK & COVER PHOTO & DESIGN
Melanie Gendron
melaniegendron999@gmail.com

AUTHOR PHOTO
Betsy Snider

FIRST EDITION

Library of Congress Control Number: 2020949858

ISBN: 9781421836799

This book is dedicated to the memory of
two dear friends and mentors,
Barbara Homans (1928 — 2018) and
Sister Celine Metzgar, H.M. (1932 — 2019)

Thanks to my siblings who always support me,
to Kathryn Tolbert who keeps me grounded,
to Diane Frank who guides me through
the tangled paths of my poems and
to Pam Bernard who provides
wisdom, insight and a fresh look.

Acknowledgements

Sinister Wisdom: The Lesbian Body,
"You Would Have Me Love" Fall, 2017

Black Magnolias: A Literary Journal,
"Long Ride Home" Summer, 2009

Carrying the Branch: Poets in Search of Peace
(Lyre Glass Press, 2017)
"Paris is Burning, November 2015"

Mud Chronicles: A New England Anthology
(Monadnock Writers' Group, 2018)
"Spring Hike"

Accepted for publication
Pandemic Puzzle Poems (Blue Light Press, 2020)
"Stones for the Dead"

Contents

Part Four — Coming Home

Part I

Ars preces

Meditations on the art of prayer by a lesbian ex-nun

i.

I have forgotten the joy of water,
my hands pulling through the black density
surrounding me, rhythmically
breathing in the chilled dawn.

Ice is a memory. Like the dreams
of dead lovers, misty ghosts skim
across the hills. Winter tucks behind
a door firmly closed.

Months unspool before me.
Summer beckons.
I am undone.

ii.

— after reading "White Owl Flies Into and Out of the Field"
by Mary Oliver

The question of god is etched
against the snow at midnight,
bare birch branches reach upward.
In the long watch, I contemplate
what waits on the other side — so much
aortal light that we are washed
out of our bones.

Or perhaps nothing, just a universe
indifferent in its cruel beauty.

iii.

Love coils between the beats of my heart.
Hope wraps around the pulsar
behind my third eye.

Dark stars bleed light at the edges.
Lovers crowd my tongue. I am silent
in the space where neurons blink
desperate notes of redemption.

Rain weighs on gold leaves.
The lake is pocked with stars
adrift in the margins of life.
I slowly sink into sand where fish walk
and god sings.

iv.

Like a mouse seeking warmth in winter,
cold lingers past all memory.

Just ahead, as the path angles west,
 a gray fox darts into the woods.
The day after a storm is a good time
to break trail, to search for wildness
that answers only the call of death,
feels the hunger that is the voice
that sings in winter, the scent
to drive beasts out into raw wind.

The shadows stir, the sun angles low
and I turn back to follow my prints home.

v.

I've taken to hiking an old path
faintly visible through strands of birch,
looking for what I lost.

Suddenly, a flash of yellow.

My father flings me skyward.

vii.

At first, we were told not to speak.
Sacred Silence was all about not saying anything
after Compline until next day's Mass.

Not speaking was the easy part.
Not allowing words to tumble out.
What's impossible is keeping silent.
Being silent prepares the heart,
keeping silent destroys the spirit.

viii.

Grace falls
thick as sunshine
in July
across my shoulders
where wings
once sprouted.

I didn't know
grace was a burden,
would leave bruises

sharp as ribs,
as the razor blade
I hide
under the box cutter
beneath
the panties
I never wear
anymore.

ix.

You would have me love
    the small of your back,
    the secret space
        where sweat collects
            under your breasts,
    the soft spot
        on the inside of your thigh
            where my tongue lingers
                to savor salt sour tang

    along the arch
        of your right foot,
  behind the lobe
        of your left ear.

I lick the scars
on your body —
        right collarbone,
            left inner wrist,
                both groins —
and breathe in
    the hollows and spaces
        where you hide
        deep inside.

And still
      it is not
            enough.

x.

I kneel on the stone floor at midnight.
My blue serge habit, purpled from harsh
soap, provides no cushion for knees scarred
by prayers and cleaning. Silence cups
my ears under my stiff headdress.

And yet, music coils around the shadows.
Cherry ribs arc overhead where my prayers
break in the flickering light of a candle.

xi.

Inside the hollows of my shoulder blades,
crystals lodge, bone shatters on rock.
My heart skitters, all restless heat.
Snow covers me with a thin nightgown.

xii.

My wings grew back last night
while I flew through storms,
a great wind across the water.

I wake wrapped in feathers,
bones grown from nubs
left behind in my fall from grace.

I fall off the edge
and wait for god to lift me.

xiii.

Trees are prayers the earth sings.
Their notes echo from the vault
of sky while empty branches
gather buds from deep inside.

Like chant at midnight, stark trees reach up
toward a sun filled with promise.
Soon robins add glissandos
of hope, spring peepers ring
from the marshes, crickets chirp
as they emerge from the damp earth.

xiv.

High on Gove Hill, water springs
under winter frost.
The trail masks perils under snow,
uneven with hidden rocks,
roots of white pines pushing upward.

I use my poles to gauge risk,
skitter across ice.
Tracks of deer and rabbits,
squirrels and mice tell stories
of hunger, of cold, of need.

Beneath my boots, water runs
clear and silent down the hill
to find its rest in the lake. At the crest,
I turn back, follow my steps home.

xv.

Somewhere an owl screams.
Ice forms on my spine.
Fear, the night's quietest sound,
wraps its bony arms around my body.

xvi.

At the center is nothing, an eyelash
curled into light. Clouds skim
across the sky as I hike Coffin Hill,
the sharp slap of guns echoing
in the forest where deer blend
into fallen leaves and birch limbs.

Emptiness gathers its skirts.

xvii.

The wafer is thin, dry,
just as it was when I thought
god would melt on my tongue —
food for those who hunger
for the divine. Maybe god
tastes of ash, smoke
born on the wind.

Part II

Blood Bound

Her Heart is a Map of the World

My mother has not opened her eyes for days.
I stand guard at the bed, watch her hands
scrabble at the thin cotton blanket, listen
to the shudder of her breath as it slows.

I whisper my story in my mother's ear.

On My Parents' 80th Anniversary

My eyelashes freeze together
in the wasted landscape.
The shovel rings against the frozen ground,
as I move fresh snow around the piles
that reach up the windows.

I watch the air take form,
become solid as my fingers
thrust into orange mittens.
Snow becomes the quilt
my grandmother made from scraps
eighty years ago.
She gave it to my mother
on her wedding day.
Now, it drapes my bed.

I curl under its weight.
I know spring will come
as it always does,
whether I am here or not.

Spring at the Lake

The ice disappeared overnight this year.
Usually, it drifts with no purpose,
growing thinner and darker, moves
restlessly, as if hearing the call of geese
on a distant wind. But this year,
it left Sunday night. And the mergansers
came on Monday, gliding and ducking
for fish newly vulnerable below the surface.

On the far shore, my mother stands among the white pines,
hidden under layers of memory. The ghosts
of her children call her from the middle of the lake
where they float on old inner tubes
resurrected from the tractor now atilt in the field.

In the evening, I feed a single black duck
as I sit on the faded blue Adirondack chair
and listen for my mother's voice to sing me asleep.

Life is running past us now.

If I close my eyes, I watch a girl,
hair shocked by sun, skin toasted
and spotted with mosquito bites,
scrapes on bare knees and elbows.

She tumbles down a long hill,
her legs churn as she jumps
into the pond, water brown
and murky under a hazy sun.

Just like her, my time summersaults
through the air, the world bent
as past leaps into future, present
hidden in the woods just beyond the water.

I fly above the patchwork of meadows
and pastures, until all is blurred,
my sight dark at the edges, silence falls
with absolute clarity.

Three Wishes

When I was a child, I wanted a horse.
We lived on an old farm, with a barn
with stalls, and a hayloft.
I spent hours sitting on that horse,
high above the ground, untouchable.
But my mother said no.

When I was in college, I dreamed
of the perfect lover, whose curves
matched mine, whose lips were soft,
whose breasts filled my hands
and whose touch burned.
But good girls didn't french-kiss.

Now, fantasies of horses
and lovers drift like clouds in summer.

My third wish is an easy death
that comes in the night,
wrapped around the sound
of my mother's lullaby.

The Confession of a Fallen Catholic

What happens when the bed-rock disappears,
ice breaking way in March, the sun
and wind open chasms of empty space
where nothing can hold, where I become
unburdened by wings and flight?

The ground opens, the sky folds into clouds,
water hurtles and I am a rock
falling from the cliff into a sea fathoms deep.

Suddenly, feathers soft
as my mother's hands on her death bed
wrap my bones into light, free me aloft.
I sing the dawn awake.

Early Summer Dream

The rain falls in silver sheets.
I gather it around my shoulders
as I stride into the forest.
Today is the day.
I feel my mother lean
against my breast,
hear my sisters keening.

I am luminous among the hemlocks,
my skin soft with water, all edges
blurred as I curl into the ferns.
I leave as I arrived,
wet with promise.

Siblings

We grew up in the trenches, in the battle of family life
where blood seeped from skinned knees,
where bruises blossomed from sharp elbows
thrust in unwary sides, where blind eyes were cast
and secrets buried like dirty socks under the bed.

We were spread out over 16 years,
leisurely, as though time had no end or purpose.
Through the great distance of years
and the intimate space of a ramshackle farm house,
we grew like the beans planted every spring.

One by one, we disappeared into the wild
world that sprang up beyond the woods.
To the west coast, to the east coast,
to a bloody war on another continent.
But we always returned to bury our dead.

And soon, we will gather to bury one of us.
Or not. Chasms form, a vast abyss
separates a family riven by shame and silence.
A great wave of stillness washes me clean.

Of Eggplants and Elephants

"Quick," her voice breathes from the phone,
"I need to be grateful for something
that begins with an e. Suggestions?"
I start to laugh, she responds
with a chuckle. Her newest exercise
to slow her racing mind. Think of things,
not people or places, but objects
of her gratitude starting with A
and ending with Z. She's stuck on E.

I suggest, "ex-nuns" since she can't use
Elizabeth. Because I am the only ex-nun,
or indeed any nun, that she's known,
she laughs. "I'm serious," she says.

So am I. But ex-nuns must move on
from daily contemplation of the divine.
I learned years ago to hide the scars
of fallen angels, so I suggest eggplants
or perhaps elephants. "Elephants it is,"
she replies, satisfied to have found
gratitude in an animal she's never met.

And I am happy to think of Babar and Celeste,
my mother's voice drifting over me.

advice to my 14 year old self

She grows into a body she doesn't recognize,
with its new angles and strange bulges.
Her body of clay is being sculpted at night
when she dreams of Sister Andrew
and the refuge of the convent.

She is taller than most of the boys
at Assumption. She wonders
if she will be the tallest student
in her new high school, which only
has girls, which is in Cleveland,
which is two bus trips away.

In the faded picture, she stands alone.
The shy smile, long legs,
arms angled around her body
as though she doesn't know what to do
with herself, how to hold this body
when it doesn't listen to her, how to hide
from prying eyes and hot breath.

Don't worry, I want to tell her.
"All shall be well, and all shall be well,
and all manner of thing shall be well."

A Dream of Helixes

The sheets are tangled with sweat,
hair spiked from the pillow.
Buried in a dream, I scream in silence.

It is a nightmare that follows me
like the horse Mr. Tubbs kept
in the field down the dirt road
that ended nowhere, a ravine
left behind when the strip miners finished.

Now seventy years beckon me
into a future with the mare
nudging in my back, in its quest
for sugar, for a rub.

In my dream, I hear my mother:
"Don't go back to sleep."

The scar that will not heal.

Every morning, blood wells
from 40 year old scars,
memories like great toads,
tongues flicking in the dim light.

The scars came long after I grew up,
past the time of redress, born of anger
and shame, and razor blades honed to hurt.

Blood still drips from wounds wrapped
in gauze, skin worn thin, bruises
blossom from injuries recollected.

Raggedy Ann perches naked and torn
on a stained mattress. The child weeps
in silence. Rain drips from trees heavy with leaves.

Memory Box

— after reading "Never Give All The Heart" by W.B. Yeats

I.

The hayloft has no hay in it,
no horses in the stalls
and the small tack room is bare.

Ghosts of children gather in corners,
debris forgotten over decades
while life plays itself on a movie screen.

Time folds in origami squares,
the past repeats into future pain
while today stands still as a mountain.

The old woman stares at the wall.
She is deaf and dumb and blind with love
for she gave all her heart and lost.

II.

In the corner of an old chicken coop,
the wind blows shadows of children,
limned in charcoal.

Old movies shown on sheets
now ripped, faces flicker
across the visual cortex.

Deep in the folds, pain lingers.
The old woman holds out her hand
to catch the memory of the child.

III.

The old farmhouse now empty,
charred walls open to rain,
ashes form thick paste on black earth.

Bedrooms appear in the shadows.
Closet doors swing shut
while pictures curl in corners.

Oak trees bow, leaves float away.
The old woman climbs on bent limbs
to fly past the moon hidden in smoke.

IV.

The lake is a perfect mirror
in late October, still as the child
with hands curled into fists.

Images float across the lake
like mist in early June, a man
and the child in a bathing suit

sitting in the sand together,
his fingers resting on her thigh
while he pulls her closer.

Wind flutters, gray skies open.
The old woman crosses a bridge
to the child who waits in shadow.

A Dream of the Fall

I walk to the railroad trestle,
abandoned and listing but still
attached at each end over the gorge.

I found it last week on a ramble
through the woods, sugar maples
in full red salute, paper white birch
wrapped in gold, oaks turning copper.

The trestle appeared like a light
at the end of a leafy tunnel,
bright, vanishing into the sky.

Today is the day that I will embrace
the future that god has laid before me
since I was a child bound to my uncle
in silence and shame. Seventy years
of fetters wrapped around my scarred wrists.

The sun wraps its warmth around me,
leaves flutter good-byes, one drowsy bee
snuggles against a faded rose.

I step off the rotted ties,
arms out to clasp the air.

Of Strings and Helixes

I worry my mother's pearls
like the rosary beads I wore
around my waist
in another life
when time was bound
by bells and prayers.

The pearls are round
as the plump peas
I picked from the garden
in another life
when time was measured
in sunrise and sunset.

They drape my collarbone
warm as my newborn daughter
curled against my breast
in another life
when time was gauged
by sleep and wails.

Last night, the string broke.
Lives scattered, rolling down stairs
steep as cliffs, frightful and sheer.
In the morning,
the cat plays with a stray pearl.

Mirror, Mirror

The only mirrors in the convent were in the bathrooms,
where we would brush our teeth and wash our faces.
Our bodies covered by voluminous habits
of blue serge, and white headdresses and coifs, we had
no need of mirrors. We all looked the same,
we were all called sisters and we learned how to walk
in unison without setting our rosary beads clacking.

I grew unaccustomed to checking myself in the mirror,
even decades after I left the convent and the habit far behind.
I have a mirror in the bathroom, and an old one
from my grandmother's bathroom that now hangs
in the hall. Because my vision is wearing out,
like the rest of me, and I wear my glasses just for reading,
I glance in the bathroom mirror and see only
the young girl who thought she was called by god.

Brother With No Name

He inhabits my dreams, a ghost
who will not be appeased.
He surrounds himself with family,
loving wife and daughters.
They do not see the skull
lurking under flesh grown heavy
in prison, nor smell the whiff
of brimstone carried in his clothes.

I am broken under his weight.

Time Past

I curl under a hemlock at midnight.
Stars prick holes in the velvet black sky.
In the distance, the sound of a great sigh
echoes against the shoulders of a mountain.

I wait for my mother to gather elderberries
black as pitch near the deep forest gloom.
I press my hand against the earth,
feel the rock move under my ribs.

I circle once, then my wings flare
red and orange in the waning air.

Part III

Sisters and Brothers in Arms

A Nun Laid to Rest in Spring

Beneath the patience of the bark,
sap wakens. Red buds clothe
branches long bare under winter frost.

Leaves from last fall pile around
the open hole among the tombstones.

A whisper echoes the chapel bell
that calls Celine to prayer, to god, to silence.

Adrift

Barbara does not have much time.
We do not speak of it aloud,
our eyes glance sideways
as if the truth would laser our skin.
Her solid certitude has given way
to frailty, her voice as soft
as a rose petal wet with morning.
The chemo has sapped fortitude
built over ninety years of life.

I would hold her close, but ours
is not a friendship built on touch,
but rather constructed from words
that spill past the solid dams
constraining us. But not now,
not with the raven hunched
on her shoulder. We tend to silence.

For Orlando

I carry 49 bodies on my shoulders.
The weight bows me into the ground.
Voices whisper in my ear —
"Help me!" "He's coming." "Mommy,
I'm going to die." "I love you."
The smallest bone echoes
with grief. Memories etched
in the corner of my eyes replay
on the screen that hangs in my mind.

When I swim, it is the beat of my heart
that I hear, the pulse of life carries me
across the lake and the sun edges
past clouds to mirror red on the surface.

Death stalks me in the shadows.
I will meet my broken sisters and brothers
on the shores of Acheron.

Ginling Girls College — Nanking, 1937

for Minnie Vautrin

Charred bones sing to me at night,
young girls play harps, strings taut
as crossbows aimed at my heart.

In the courtyard, ten thousand
gather, flames flicker on walls
pockmarked with scars of war.

Boots pound outside, loud
as drums sounding the alarm
when hounds hunt the fox.

They people my dreams.
Eyes hollow. Bones leached
by sun, weighted under chains.
Thousands howl against bitter winds
that batter walls scarred
by bullets and bayonets.

I stand alone in the whirlwind
to name the faceless, to bear
witness to the slain, to shame
those mute watchers hidden
in the shadows of their lives.

Death comes wrapped in capsules,
swallowed in dark silence.

Long Ride Home

She stands at the bus stop
on a drizzly December evening.
It's been a long day, the store
was full of fussy women
in white gloves and pill box hats,
demanding that she find
the proper sheets for them,
the right colors, the exact
blend of cotton and linen.

In the gray light, a bus looms.
The doors spring open as she
slowly ascends the steps,
moves behind the line,
set about 4 rows back,
and gingerly sits on the aisle,
next to a man in a trilby hat.
Her feet throb and her shoulders ache.

The driver tells them to move back.
The front is full and they need to move
back. The man next to her stands,
she shifts into the aisle as he
walks past her. Determination
covers her like a quilt on a winter night.
She sits back in her seat,
moves to the window and waits.

Later, after she's been arrested,
photographed, fingerprinted, put

in jail, released; after a city boycotts
its buses and her face is as familiar
as Abe Lincoln's, she's asked whether
she didn't move because she was just
too tired. She replies, "The only tired
I was, was tired of giving in." Sometimes,
the universe disturbs the woman.

How To Be a Woman in Sierra Leone

In memory of Fannyann Eddy, lesbian activist
1974-2004

"O Jesus burning on the lily cross/
O night, rawhead and bloodybones night/
O night betrayed by darkness not its own"

"Night, Death, Mississippi" by Robert Hayden

The floor smelled of oranges,
unnoticed until she was forced
face first in the dirt. The sharp tang
of fruit mingled with the sweat
of her fear.

Hours later, after they moved
the body to the morgue,
technicians found rinds
of clementines crushed
by her feet as they beat
a bid for freedom.

At trial, the five men boasted
that she died smiling
as their cocks rammed home
the truth — all a dyke needs
is a good fuck.

We Are All Refugees

1. Greece

Jihan Sheikh Mohammed settles in the tent,
scarf pulled close,
tattered shawl draped over narrow shoulders.
Her children are scattered,
drowned in frigid seas,
cast upon frozen shores,
lost in the firestorm
that brought her to this meager island.
She fingers her beads,
knows that a merciful god
is a tale told to small children
huddled in the dark.
She throws the bones of her ancestors
into the sea that left her blind.

2. Standing Rock Reservation

In the tipi built like her grandfather's,
Bobbi Jean Three Legs squats before the fire.
Outside, winds howl and sleet taps against the hide.
If she squints her eyes, she can see buffalo
mounded on the ground, 200 years past.
For over a year, she has gathered
the scattered youth, driven to alcohol,
drowned in dreams, cast upon lonely plains.
She serves a spirit plate,
rattles the beads, prays to the Great Mystery.

3. Cleveland Ohio

In the darkening room, Irene McGraw sits,
her rusty hair stiff as a wire brush

and mutters, "You make your own luck."
She remembers the boat that brought
the ten of them - her three brothers,
five sisters and widowed mother
worn threadbare by the journey -
from County Cork to Cleveland.
The famine killed the father she never knew
and left the rest of them, red-haired wraiths
wrapped in tattered cotton shirts and pants.
They left Ireland for scraps and worked
at McGorray's funeral home, tending the dead
and driving the hearse with its heavy load.
She never talked of those blasted fields,
of the dirt in the cemetery, of all her dead
siblings, of how she planned her life
with only three children to mourn her.
She will die as she lived, silent, thin-lipped
and taking her secrets into the dark.

Lesbos, December 2015

The bodies wash ashore
cast off by an indifferent sea.
I stand on a beach littered
not with purple sarongs
but with orange life vests
no longer needed.

This is not how I dreamed
of Greece. The heat is leached
by a wind north from Sweden.
Ice crystals form above waves
that pound relentlessly
on a shingle of sand.

Sappho waits to greet me with a pillow of stone.

A Black Abaya Floats On the Aegean

Life is pared to its bare necessities.
An extra pair of shoes, one bra,
two cotton panties, a gray sweatshirt.

It wasn't always this way.
A home with rooms once stretched
to sky, until the bomb exploded
and the future became orange
life vests strapped on children.

Now hope threads a heart broken
on gray stones, a flat shingle of beach
where open hands reach out in the dark.

Rural America

— in memory of James Byrd, Jr.

The moon leaches blood black in its light.
Drained of context, blood pools in the grit
scattered by broken bones, as the body
is dragged five miles and abandoned,
shattered cheek kissing asphalt.

Dreams of dead men and young boys,
girls left torn in the dust, a world cast adrift
in madness. Blue bottle flies feast
while orchids bloom under a full moon.

The Perfect Offering of an Old Woman

I stare at the shattered ceiling,
the mirror where the shards
of my soul collect dust
and god whistles off-key.

Water drips like a chant,
the pulse beats through my heart
and I fall, hard and blind as a diamond.

Howls echo off the hills.
The earth is riven with cracks.
Heat calls to the hawk
and the falconer's glove is rent.

Blood fills the blue tub.
The nylon reel tugs the lure,
the hook imbeds in my flesh
and I am thrown to the sky.

Behind Crab Nebula, on the far
side of a black hole, light streams
through the ceiling. I close
my eyes.

Paris is Burning, November 2015

The earth pitches over.
Planes disappear.
The arc of blue stretches to heaven.

Far away, bombs explode
light into potsherds of civilization
that drift back into the dust of the universe.

My knees crack, unused to the hard stone
of faith, the sure knowledge of Truth,
the priests chant in the pines.

I wrap myself in the shroud of doubt
and walk to the lip of the abyss.
Stars shower my shoulders in luminance.

Stones for the Dead

— a reflection on George Floyd

A stone is placed on his neck,
just at the point where his spine
holds his head upright.
But he is on the ground, face in the dirt,
like so many before him.
Hot asphalt and the grit of sand
left by tires and boots
cradle his cheek. In pain,
he finds his mother
caressing his head, her tears
washing the stain of death
from his closed eyes.

He is borne away on the river
where the boatman lays
his broken body, now ready
to rise.

Dialogue with Selene

How did you gather our broken-off volcanos
to create your craters of stone?

On your far side, is there a face
or do you weep for your lost children?

When did you learn to reflect our light
rather than absorb us into your dark?

What will happen as distance between us
grows larger and gravity fractures along our edge?

Where will we be when the center flies apart?

Part IV

Coming Home

I Seek My Name

In the dark night, it came —
the call echoed
between the ribs, pain
etched on the slate
of my soul. A name
framed by the slant of light
on the horizon.

Years passed. My body grew
accustomed to torment.
I was clothed in a habit
of woe, wrapped by beads
of grief, inconsolable —
nameless in my rage.

Until the day I understood.

Requiem for an Ex-Nun

The weight of sin lies heavy
across my shoulders. The albatross
cannot fly; its wings are broken.
I did not think my life would end
this way: alone, save for the bird
and the shell cracked open at my feet.

Dawn breaks with a wash of blood.

Kyrie eleison buried deep
in the anvil of my ear.

Flight

Fireflies flicker
at the edge of dogwoods
long after the flowers drift away.

My mother's hands are cracked
and bloody from the garden,
weeds overtaken the roses.

I cling to the top of an apple tree,
hidden, alone in my perch among the phoebes.
No one looks up. I am safe.

The horizon thins in the distance,
a line smudged
with the encroaching night.

I know I will run away soon.

Ice Out on the Lake

Every year, ice begins its dance with water
by thinning, by moving, by wearing away
the solid mass until a leaf goes through,
touches the water that hides for months.
The lake sloughs off its dead skin.

My mind circles the ice, eddies past
the old dam and remains of the mill.
Nothing is familiar underwater. I breathe
through gills now opening under the scars.
My legs become fins, my eyes are lidless.

Death on a Sunday Afternoon

Her eyes drift over my left shoulder.
I wonder what she sees.
Perhaps morphine induces visions,
her father standing at the foot
of her bed, her mother crying softly
in his arms, her aunt weaving
silently in the corner.

There is nothing to say.
Goodbye, friend. I will not see
you again on this side
of the divide, between the smell
of a body giving up its breath
and the whisper of god.

She will not die alone, unshriven.
The soft murmuring of her daughters,
of the priest in his collar and purple stole
will carry her beyond this room
into the light that sheds no shadows.

Counterpoint

Day of wrath, oh day of mourning.
Day fulfills the prophet's warning.
Heaven and earth in ashes burning.

In my dream, I sing Benedictus
with my sisters, chant rising
to the rafters like incense
in the dark before dawn.

We rise to song, call and response
lifting us from our narrow beds.
We dress behind sheets,
don blue habits and white veils.

The Angelus rings at noon.
We gather in the chapel
to remember god become flesh
and the virgin who bore him.

Nunc dimitis follows us
along the narrow path to bed,
light and glory now fading
as we wrap ourselves in song.

I Hear the Roses Sing

In the early morning, after I swim
across the lake, I hear the roses
sing to butterflies, call them
to sip nectar, to carry pollen
from bud to bud.

I once sang Lauds
with my sisters, breaking
our silence in song that reached
the arched cherry wood rafters
of the chapel. Now the roses
and butterflies sing in counterpoint
above the trills of the phoebe.

At mid-day, all is silent.
The heat stuns us all
into quiet genuflection.
We wait for the long shadows of evening
to whisper us home.

The Chapter of Faults

The day slid past almost unnoticed,
another random Tuesday among hundreds
even thousands already ticked off.
Surely I am too old to keep up
with the rituals of youth, the toting
of one's faults, what doesn't even rise
to the level of sin, what can remain
unshriven in the eyes of the god
I no longer recognize.

And yet, I can hear the clacking
of beads, the rustling of long serge skirts,
gathered as the sisters sit in silence
and wait for the call to prayer,
hunched over our darning, eyes cast down.

Every Tuesday, we spend an hour
recounting transgressions against
rules of sisterhood, the pact joined
when we robed ourselves in blue.
One by one, we kneel on the linoleum,
knees padded only by our long habits,
and confess our failures to each other.

Decades have passed, but I remember
the hard floor, the unyielding regard
of my sisters, the movement of needles
repairing holes worn in habits thinned
by harsh soap, the coughs and murmurs.
I am no longer bound by such minutiae,
no rules bind me to those long forgotten sisters.

And yet, every January, on the first day
of the new year, I recall the weekly circle,
the drone of voices and the gray linoleum floor,
flecked with faint slivers of blue and green.

Motorcycles and Ducks

The ice finally went out
late Friday night. I spent
the day, watching it drift
back and forth, until it stacked
up on the eastern shore.

The ducks flew in earlier,
grateful for open water
They dunked their heads
and flapped their wings, free
of the burden of flight.
They spent the day chivvying
the ice eastward until it disappeared
from my sight, black floes
dipping under blue water.

On Saturday, the lake shook
off its shackles, waves
glittering in the sun.

I hear the sound of motorcycles
rumble past the lake,
and the ducks talking
to each other, mergansers
to mallards, wood ducks to
black ducks, baffle heads
to loons, the honk of geese.

As I slip into the lake
for the first swim of the season,
ducks ride their motorcycles
in circles to the center of the world.

A Day in June

Sweat gathers between my breasts
as I hike to the top of Potato Hill.
Mosquitoes descend,
a thick cloud of hunger.
Days of rain make the path slick
under my boots, rocks wet and muddy.
My poles keep me upright
as I navigate downhill. Jeff the donkey
brays as I stride past his field.
I wave my pole to him and keep moving.

Finally, I run into my shed, don my black speedo,
its pink and orange straps faded over the years,
and jump off the dock into water
still holding ice deep within.

Silence spreads its wings,
as I dive into the center
where nothing holds.

Lakeside in September

The great blue heron perches
on the metal boat stanchion,
a long ogee almost invisible
in its deliberate stillness.

The pickerel weed is dying
along the edges of the lake.
The angle of the sun shifts.
Fish begin their slow descent.

I watch the heron from my dock
for an hour, trying to mirror
its focus, its ferocity, its hunger.
But honeybees distract me.

Their insistent buzz drums in my ears
as they search in plants tattered
and drooping with faded blossoms
for nectar already plundered.

I look again to the heron.
Not a feather flutters,
nor does the head dip
or the talon flex.
Until it rises with majesty
and dives into the lake.

I am left alone on the dock
as the light fades over the mountain.

January

Rain clogs snow-filled gutters,
blows against windows,
slides across icy paths,
beats snow piles into submission.

My mind moves across a landscape
pockmarked with failure, scarred
by memories of razor blades.

The flood rises in the field,
gathers snow and ice, limbs
broken under the weight
of the past, bodies buried under leaves.

I break into brittle shards,
transparent in the dim light
that creeps across pine floors
worn to thin edges by dogs long dead.

New Hampshire in February

Dark creeps past hemlocks,
rolls under fences,
climbs cliffs of ice,
cocoons snow thick with rime,
then lodges against my breast.

Every morning, light blossoms,
sings anthems of praise,
rests atop white birches
shorn by winter's winds,
hangs cotton in blue sky.

But night comforts me,
its pulse beating under cover.
Shadows wait for the hum of bees
deep in hives to wake me.

I dream of death

No incense, no rattling beads,
no wailing, no gnashing of teeth.
No children gathered around
as I curl up on plastic sheets.
A scarf tossed aside
after a night on the town.

Books stacked in towers
against the wall, newspapers
scattered on bare pine floors.
Poems stuck into nooks
where dreams of a baby faded.

Spring Hike

The trail is riddled with hollow spaces
where ice releases its grasp underground
and the thin membrane of earth collapses into itself.

Yesterday, Katmandu shifted ten feet south
while I hiked along rocks and hillocks
that sank into mud as my feet grabbed purchase.

The earth trembles as ice thins,
as plates crash, as magma boils,
as polarities shift deep in the core.

Tonight, I inspect a sky written
in a language that translates nebulae
into stars drifting southward across
the hollow space of dark matter.

End Times

Voices carry across water
through the thick air.
Laughter echoes on distant hills.

I lay flat on the thin mattress.

All five of us siblings used to swing
in the rope hammock, like puppies
curled around Rusty until she ran
under the school bus one day.

Clouds gather in my mind.

We sprawled in fields
among the Queen Anne's lace
and picked out dragons and wizards
floating against an azure sky.
We walked through the stream
behind the barn every day,
abandoning shoes and socks.

The sheet is lifted over my slack face.

I dive deep into the lake,
touch the sandy bottom
and surge to the surface
aflame.

About the Author

Betsy Snider is a retired attorney who lives on a lake in rural New Hampshire with the ghosts of her many cats and dogs. When she is not swimming or hiking, she writes poetry and has volunteered as a CASA Guardian ad Litem for abused and neglected children.

She was first published in the ground-breaking anthology, *Lesbian Nuns: Breaking Silence* (Naiad Press, 1985). She is a winner of the 2015 Blue Light Book Award for her book of poems, *Hope is a Muscle* (Blue Light Press, 2015). Her poetry has been published in a variety of journals and anthologies, most recently in *The Mud Chronicles* (Monadnock Writers' Group, 2018); *Carrying the Branch* (Glass Lyre Press, 2017); *The Lesbian Body* (Sinister Wisdom, Fall 2017); *Amore: Love Poems* (Imagination Press, 2016); *Our Last Walk* (University Professors Press, 2016); *River of Earth and Sky: Poems for the 21st Century* (Blue Light Press, 2015); *Poet Showcase* (Hobblebush Press, 2015); and *Love Over 60: an anthology of women's poems* (Mayapple Press, 2010).

www.ingramcontent.com/pod-product-compliance
Lightning Source LLC
Chambersburg PA
CBHW032028090426
42741CB00006B/771